Written After a Massacre in the Year 2018

Also by Daniel Borzutzky

In the Murmurs of the Rotten Carcass Economy
The Book of Interfering Bodies
Lake Michigan
Memories of My Overdevelopment
The Performance of Becoming Human

Written
After a
Massacre
in the
Year 2018

Daniel Borzutzky

COFFEE HOUSE PRESS
Minneapolis
2021

The cover artwork is a detail from *Quipu Menstrual*
(Nevado del Plomo, Chile), copyright © 2016 by Cecilia Vicuña.
Photograph is by James O'Hern. Image is courtesy of the artist and
Lehmann Maupin, New York, Hong Kong, and Seoul.

The author photograph is by Patri Hadad and is courtesy of the University of
Arizona Poetry Center, copyright © 2018 by the Arizona Board of Regents.

Coffee House Press books are available to the trade through our primary distribu-
tor, Consortium Book Sales & Distribution, cbsd.com or (800) 283-3572. For per-
sonal orders, catalogs, or other information, write to info@coffeehousepress.org.

Coffee House Press is a nonprofit literary publishing house. Support from pri-
vate foundations, corporate giving programs, government programs, and gener-
ous individuals helps make the publication of our books possible. We gratefully
acknowledge their support in detail in the back of this book.

LIBRARY OF CONGRESS CATALOGING-IN-PUBLICATION DATA

Names: Borzutzky, Daniel, author.
Title: Written after a massacre in the year 2018 / Daniel Borzutzky.
Identifiers: LCCN 2020039021 (print) | LCCN 2020039022 (ebook) |
    ISBN 9781566895996 (hardcover) | ISBN 9781566896054 (epub)
Subjects: LCGFT: Poetry.
Classification: LCC PS3602.O79 W75 2020 (print) | LCC PS3602.O79 (ebook) |
    DDC 811/.6--dc23
LC record available at https://lccn.loc.gov/2020039021
LC ebook record available at https://lccn.loc.gov/2020039022

Acknowledgments
Thanks to the editors of the following journals and venues for publishing poems
from this book: Academy of American Poets (Poem-a-Day), *Big Other, Blackbox
Manifold, Boston Review, 580 Split, Georgia Review, Guernica, Harvard Review,
Hyperallergic, Jewish Currents, Kenyon Review, New York Public Library: Poem in
Your Pocket Day, A Public Space,* the *Rumpus,* and *West Branch.*

PRINTED IN CANADA
28 27 26 25 24 23 22 21   1 2 3 4 5 6 7 8

To Tree of Life and Pittsburgh

To the love that survives

To Chicago and Santiago

To the love that survives

To those who migrate

To the love that survives

To those murdered by white supremacists

To the love that survives

To those murdered by the state

To the love that survives

For all of us   we break and are broken

—

For Raúl Zurita

For Cecilia Vicuña

My heroes in art

CONTENTS

Written After a Massacre in the Year 2018

The
Blankest
of
Times

Managed Diversity

Through predictive analytics I understood the inevitability of the caged-up babies

They keep coffins at the border for when the refugees get too far from home

How many bodies can we fit in a tent or a swimming pool

We can live without the unknown in front of us if we keep enough babies in cages

The cardboard box sleeps one kid comfortably

Two is snug   efficient   recommended in times of austerity

Relational values change in relation to market sentiments

This is the danger of having too much access to illegal bodies

Let's pretend the illegal bodies are bankers

Let's stick all the bankers in cages

Let's shove shit in their mouths

Let's pretend they are eating cryptocurrency

Let's create a crisis let's induce inflation

Let's undervalue the cost of their bodies

I dream of an economy where one arrested immigrant is replaced with one dead banker

I am not responsible for my dreams rather I am responsible for what I do with my dreams

When the sleep medication wears off I am alone with the machines that watch me

The global economy brightens my room with the surveillance of my rotten assets

Systemic Risk

But the people in the dining room
Are busy being born and dying
　　　　—Os Mutantes, "Panis et Circenses"

You can analyze systemic risk
according to how many bodies live or die

If the system fails
the broken bodies
become invisible and/or hypervisible

The people are being born and dying

They are enacting the invisibility
of the security system
through the exhibition of their naked bodies

I eat corrupted data
to keep my skin
from becoming transparent

I would rather be
a defect of culture
than a defect of data or character

What is not observed
grows more visible
in relation to the strength of the surveillance

It's better to deprive
a few million people of food
than to pull the plug on the global economy

If the consumers don't want your product
then teach them the meaning of love

Poem #1022

There is not much excess
and what there is is barely perceptible
the blank ones disappear from our vision
no one notices until
there is a dramatic decrease in surplus value

the war is born
and the blank ones disappear again
but really their disappearance is subjective
some see no one
while others see everyone

for some the extermination of the cancer is
inseparable from the decreation of the city
others associate the decreation
with an unstoppable flow of leakage
while others associate the decreation
with falling rates of profit
and the barely perceptible
        appearance of the human body

out of the dead refugee sprouts
                a breathing poem

out of the dead soldier sprouts
                a breathing poem

out of the dead city sprouts
                a breathing poem

but when the city disappears
                so do the poems

and when the poems disappear
                the dead are assassinated

picture a heart covered in dust
and picture a poem sprouting out of it

picture a heart covered in dust
and picture a child chasing it

picture a bullet that kills a child
and picture the soldier who tosses the child into the sea

the soldier kisses the earth and says
it's not my fault the people are being born and dying

the pastor calls out the names of the children to the congregants

to each name they respond
dead

Day #423

The beach is burning in the middle of the city and they tell

Us the lake is not dead but we know it has

Disappeared into the chemical blankness and

The sand is full of disease and

The water is full of petroleum and the water is full of bodies

With cadmium and arsenic in their ears

They have lead in their mouths they

Are falling out of the sky or they are bones in the earth

They are clinging to something they are clinging to each other

They are clinging to the air to the trees to the breath to the night

And you   are a wounded shoulder in the hypnosis of the emergency

You are shrapnel and inexhaustible love

You wear a mold-mask of shame

You see shame in the growth of the willow trees in the locust trees in the
red cedars

Your bones are martyrs and on the other

Side of the beach there is water but you can't see it

They will not let you near it and the waves are frozen

And you feel them

Like fat or hair or dead skin on your body

And there is the irritating hum of time and death

And the living who are dying of so much living

Of so much time and death

They are searching for life they are ghosting the ghosts who chant

Life Life like a curse word a forbidden word a disease word

And you want to see the lake again but they say you need the right code

The right mask the right space suit

And you want to see your child again but you need

An illusion a canticle an executive order

A cheek a chin a tomb a monument to the earth

A monument to the hysteria of the afternoon a monument to the rhythm

Of the sand a monument to the disappearance of the bodies who are
breaking

In some other lake   who are breaking on some other beach

Who are rioting in some other death march

The translators of the silence do not know how to translate the translators

Of the sand and in the frustration that grows between them there is
something

So ordinary   a corpse so ordinary that no one wants to disturb it

No one comes to appraise it

No one knows how much it costs or where it has been

Fabricated

It is Day #423 and the sky has

Disappeared into another sky and the beach is shrieking

The shriek of a thousand broken shoulders and I am dying

From too much life in the blankness that

Unravels into the economy of a beating a burning the guilt of this innocent lung

The shame of this atrophied bone

This bloodied body this bloodied child

This blank that consumes the image of how you understand who you are

Which is wrapped up in the image of how I understand who I am

And you don't want to die today but you might and I

Don't want to be alone today and I don't want to die

From so much life it has given me so much

To all of us we break we are broken we are

Little imitations of our corpses of eternity don't wait for us to die

It is Day #423 and shame covers my body with grief and

Grief covers my body with shame

Only twenty-three people died here yesterday and I was not one of them

And today and tomorrow and tomorrow and tomorrow and today

I will not be one of them and shame will cover my body and grief will

Live in my face and shamegrief will form in my teeth

Griefshame will blow air into my mouth and I won't die alone today

I'll eat bread I'll eat rice and kiss my child and say thank you thank you thank you

To salt and to sweat and to boredom let

Peace explode on my body I am alive and condemned and undone

Wall

They build the wall because they need privacy
It is a curtain wall with a dead load and a wind load and a seismic load
        and a blast load
It is a wall to help us find peace in a violent world
It is a wall of debt
It is a wall of accumulation
It is a private wall built with public funds
It is a sleeper wall with suspended slabs and floor joists
Poor kids are buried in the wall
When they trade bodies for petroleum they slide them through the wall
When they trade bodies for vaccines they slip them over the wall
When they trade bodies for state secrets they dig them under the wall
I've been treated very unfairly by this wall
My mouth has gone missing near this wall
My teeth have gone missing near this wall
My body has disappeared into a brick in the wall they built around the wall

I meet a slaughterer at the wall
He is kind to me
He brings me water when I am thirsty
He brings me food when I am hungry
He brings me something to kill when I am lonely
He brings me something to love when I am lonely
He brings me something empty when I need a moment of blank

There is an endless hole in the wall
I spit the wall out of my body
I hide in the wall
I become the wall
There is a murmuring ghost in the wall
The ghost of a refugee they shot against the wall
There is a foreign agent in the wall
There is an underdeveloped man in the wall
There is an underdeveloped culture in the wall
There are cheap people who wear cheap shoes and cheap shirts made in
        cheap factories protected by a very exquisite wall

There is a device in the wall
A sensor to detect movement along the wall or near the wall
There is news that comes out of the device in the wall
Bleep bleep bleep bleep   bleep bleepbleepbleepbleepbleepbleepbleepbleep
There are cannibals and pacifists in the wall
Their balls are to the wall
There is a fly on the wall
We bang our heads against the wall
There is a brick structure that divides one property from another
It is a garden wall
It is a fire wall
It is a consumption wall
It absorbs the excess bodies from the surrounding area while also
        enclosing them
It is a wall that wears many hats
It is a climbing wall with gelatinous membrane along its outer cavity
They piss money up the wall
They nail us like jelly to the wall and we dream of a wall of philanthropists
        with knives for eyes
The handwriting is on the wall
Do not climb this electrified wall
We trade cards with bureaucrat–slaughterers on the wall
They drive us up the wall
We break the fourth wall
We bounce off the wall
It is the strongest wall in the emptiest part of the valley

Risk Management

we look at our verbs and feel apathy and remorse

we look at our nouns and feel apathy and remorse

there is a mood of terror in the capitals of the industrialized democracies

we'll jump off that bridge when we get there

the economic war against the industrialized democracies is not about how many soybeans the hegemons are going to buy

the economic war is not about steel or coal or aluminum

you can lead a horse to water but you can't make it shit in the woods

the economic war can only be won in the deep verticals of state capital

the Wall Street and Washington juntas will interrupt the unification of the world's highest-performing economies

love is a sexy kind of regulatory apparatus

and when you cut off its capital and make your lover play by the rules then everybody can feel like an economic superpower

there is a mood of terror in the marketplace

should I destroy the nation-state or should I take a nap

should I destroy the foundations of our liberal democracy or should I take a nap

a bird in the hand is worth two in the bush

there is a mood of terror in the center of the city

he could not decide if he wanted to take a nap or dominate the fields of artificial intelligence industrial espionage and supercomputing

we could not decide if we wanted to take a nap or dominate the field of financial derivatives

there is a mood of exhilaration among the taxpayers

the economic war is being fought one democracy at a time

there is a mood of hunger among the proletariat

you can lead a horse to water but you can't make it destroy the means of production

there is a mood of restlessness among the political elite

the economic war is being fought one reluctant consumer at a time

you can dominate the fields of artificial intelligence and industrial espionage if you cultivate a growth mind-set and develop some political grit

there is a mood of fear in the industrialized democracies

the rising price of crude oil does not concern me when I am playing with a dog or a baby

it is not possible to give water to a horse who will not drink of its own accord

the parents who refuse to vaccinate their children   are afraid of living and afraid of dying

they think they understand how to manage their risk

there is a mood of exasperation at the Centers for Disease Control

the rising price of crude oil does not concern me when I am lifting weights or having an orgasm

it is a mistake to believe the next economic downturn will look just like the last one

there is a mood of consternation among the bankers

it is a mistake to believe the next emotional downturn will look just like the last one

there is a mood of consternation among the lovers and the investors

earnings estimates have plummeted but sales revenues continue to reach all-time highs

this is an emotional poem that communicates feelings of consternation exhilaration exasperation terror panic remorse apathy and as such it reaffirms the justification of the continuation of our lives

there is a mood of desperation among the investors

I suspect there will be more volatility but the most important thing is that we have remained in a secular market

according to Camus the only serious philosophical question is suicide but he couldn't see the forest of long-term spiritual profit because it was blocked by the short-term trees of existential panic

there is a mood of deregulation among the lovers

if you change something on the policy front   if you and your lover make a big expenditure   then decide to tighten your belts   the economy will languish and we will all be back in the muddle

there is a mood of fear among the investors

I don't think we're heading toward a recession but if we continue on the same path then we'll end up in a downward spiral from which we will never be able to recover

there is a mood of resignation among the investors

love is a sexy kind of regulatory apparatus that profits in the boldest of markets

I am tired of faith but I still believe that God can communicate through the broken mouth of a broken child

you are tired of faith but you still believe that God can communicate through the broken mouth of a broken child

we are tired of faith but we still believe that God can communicate through the broken mouth of a broken child

faith is a thing with feathers

there is a mood of hostility among the regulators

there will be more volatility but we will welcome the short-term pain if it leads to long-term gain

there is a mood of resentment in London and on Wall Street

should I strengthen my portfolio or should I destroy the nation-state

should I pursue my blood debts or should I destroy the nation-state

should I have brunch or should I redistribute the wealth

it is a mistake to underestimate the degree to which bland word choice can undermine the effectiveness of your messaging

Reality TV

He is searching for a financier

He wants to tear his eyes out

He needs a projection screen for his utopian sentiments

He needs to look into the face of an oligarch and ask him for a justification that can only amount to silence

Fuck it

Say the words anyway

How do you explain yourself to yourself when only you are listening

The border keeps inching closer

From his cage he hears the coffins being taken to the border

There are wheel loaders and laser cutters and welding machines and 3D printers and molding machines coming from Asia but no one can find the border

The trade war shifts the border from one part of the state to another

The economic embargo shifts the border from one part of the country to another

The refugee crisis shifts the border from one part of the world to another

There is a camera watching a caged-up girl as she cries for her parents

There are other children whose screams have more definition

They scream in the right language

They scream with the right intonation

The judges are unsure about which scream sounds more desperate

They analyze the echoes

They compare the tonal variations

They evaluate the modulations in pitch and volume

They assess the emotional impact on the listeners

They seek the proper language to convey the drama at the heart of the
children's screams   to turn this pain into theater worth watching

They ask the audience to clap for the child who can scream with the most
desperation

There is a scene when the journalist asks the entrepreneur   would you
live in the shacks where your workers live

The entrepreneur is offended

He thinks the question is impudent

He curses at the journalist   abruptly ends the interview and goes back
to his computer to monitor his human property

How much water do they need

Who is drinking too much water

How much disease is acceptable to pump into the product

He takes great joy in designing performance incentives for the
underdeveloped to transcend their paralysis

The underdeveloped   he says   will only develop when they learn to
escape the inescapability of their eternal underdevelopment

Lake Michigan, Scene #719

he thinks the boy's cell phone is a gun

he thinks the boy's water bottle is a gun

he thinks the cell phone is a gun and he believes in the universal right
to happiness

he thinks he can yank the cancer out of the city with his teeth

he thinks he can quarantine the contagion as part of his contractual
obligation to assert the resolute happiness of the state

he is happy when he makes the prisoners disappear into the white site

he is happy when he makes the prisoners climb to the top of the white site

he is happy when he freezes the prisoners in the block of ice they keep in
the white site

he likes to write instructional documents that say

if your body has become stuck in a block of ice   do not panic
there are many tricks you can try to get yourself unstuck
most importantly   don't die
you will be tempted to die   but don't do it
don't die   just disappear for a while into the whitest white of the white site

the authoritative bodies send detainees here when they want to nourish
them so they won't feel out of place in the discourse communities of the
bourgeoisie

they project the vision they want of the city onto the bodies they burn
and bleach

the police officer doesn't mean to shoot the boy twenty-two times it's just that when he starts shooting   the chemical compounds in his brain trigger a reflexive action

he can't think clearly because the adrenaline alters his perceptions of the real

he can't think clearly because he's convinced that a boy with a cell phone is going to shoot him

the authoritative bodies wonder   is death the proper quarantine for the contagion that covers the city   is death the proper quarantine for the bodies we should not see

the night howls and the authoritative bodies want to know what color the infected body is

what languages the infected body speaks

what languages the bodies who fabricated the infected body speak

blood type skin pigmentation hair classification

has the infected body been valuated at the appropriate price point

has the infected body been marked with the appropriate seals and signatures

they recite prayers over the infected body   how much does it cost

they slide a mask over the head of the quarantined body   how much does it cost

how much for this transfusion of native blood into foreign blood

the infected body is an ice artist with stores of foreign blood in its mouth

the infected body is an ice artist and they send it to the white site for a little nourishment but there are no free beds

and all it can do is murmur   as it travels into

the quarantined economies of the city

as it travels into   the quarantined blankness of the white site

as it travels into   the blank skies over the broken body in the excess
blankness of the white site

Murmur

what is the voice
who is the voice
when is the voice
does it murmur backwards
does it murmur with mud in its mouth
with blood in its mouth
there are blades in its mouth
dogs in its mouth
there is a nation in its mouth   a border in its mouth
there is a wall at the border in its mouth
there is a god at the border in its mouth
there is an imploding island in its mouth
an imploding economy in its mouth
there is a hemisphere in its mouth
I see the desert in its rotten carcass mouth
I see the murderers of the morning in its rotten carcass mouth
I see money   there is money   I have five dollars no I have six dollars
I need to buy the forest
I need to buy the blood trees
I need to buy the blood bush
I need more blood dogs
I have five dollars
I have six dollars
I don't know if I am hunted or if I am hunting
I eat my skin
I chew my knuckles
I suck my fingers
I hear my name in the wind
I hear the name of my god in the wind
they say I don't believe in god
they say I am secular   pagan   lacking in faith
but but   no no
but no   but no   but no
the words I use for my god are different from the words they use for their god
I can't find my fingers in the dark
I can't find my tongue in the dark

I can't find my brain in the dark
the carcass economy sustains me in the privatized darkness of dark
the mud sustains me
the blood data sustains me
the common-law blood data sustains me
the welfare state no longer sustains me
I see my slaughter mouth against the spittle of the hungry baby at my feet
I see my rat brain against the spittle of the wailing toddler with fangs at
        my feet
the toddler eating soap off my psoriasis feet
the toddler eating mud off my money feet my blood feet
the dirt toddler the wound toddler the blood toddler
there is a box a blood box a money box and they will put me in it
there is a box and when I can't buy the forest I will put myself in it
and they will ship me somewhere
because I can't afford
to build a shack in the forest
I have five dollars
I have six dollars
the conglomerate that owns the trees won't let me sit in the shade
the suit-and-tie that owns the water won't let me have a sip
I only have five dollars
I only have six dollars and I need to buy roots soil trees wind
but no
and no
but no
and no
I must smash my face into the welfare state
I must smash my face into the fist of the cop who beats me at the corner
        of Montrose and Kedzie
I must smash my face into the early American who hunts me at the corner
        of Belmont and California
I must smash my face into the language of money whose only translation
        is into more money
I must smash my face into the money drone into the health drone the
        drone of infinite scrutiny
and when they strap me into the chair and shove the peace-seeking food
        wires into my mouth

when they shove the milk wires into my mouth
when they feed me vitamins and minerals against my will
I will offer them my last five dollars to die   here take my last six dollars
        and let me die the privatized death of one who hasn't lived
and as I smash my face into the drone tomb the health tomb the tomb of
        infinite scrutiny   I will remember to smile when they love me
I will remember to smile when they feed me
to smile when they beat me
to smile when they kill me
but   and
but   and
but and but and but and

Take a
Body and
Replace
It with
Another
Body

I Explain a Few Things

They forced him to write his memoirs and covered his face in cocaine

He was an agent for the secret police or he was an agent for the mob

He believed in God   he believed in race   he believed in country

He believed that poetry was the only way to exit the space-time continuum

He tried to say I love you in a foreign language but the sentiment was lost in translation

He tried to say I love you but because he did not understand intonation he said I love lunch and she said you love what and he said I love lunch and she said you love lunch and then he understood he had said the wrong thing but he did not know how to say the right thing so he said nothing and she asked him what he wanted for lunch

I can explain

The border exploded and the people on one side of the border said   yeah   this block of ice is ours

And the people on the other side of the border said   no   this block of ice is not yours   it's ours

And the military brought coffins to the fence that separated Nation A from Nation B   the coffins were for the bodies they would kill in the battle over the block of ice

They put some bodies in the coffins but this was a low-key escalation and the bodies were not dead

They objectified the bodies

They rectified the bodies

They racialized the bodies

They overdeveloped the bodies

They privately expropriated the bodies

They hired consultants to reinvent the bodies

They transfigured the bodies

They deindustrialized the bodies

And they said if you come back tomorrow to claim the block of ice then we will have no choice but to seal your bodies in these coffins and dump you into the frozen sea

A war started

And when the war ended everything went on sale and cellular phones were half price and the people sang songs about data

They sang songs about accountability

They sang songs about market autonomy and individual choice

They sang songs about hegemonic counterhumanism and the fraudulent use of tax revenues to support public-private partnerships

They wrote the ugliest sentences imaginable

The block of ice was landfill from dissident houses they destroyed

The block of ice was bone marrow from those who died in the dissident houses they destroyed

The dissidents were now landfill under the road

The sand on the beach was an artificial construct and the women searched for the bone shards of their loved ones in the sand and the authoritative bodies said   displacement is a condition common to people from so many parts of the universe

The limits of my language   wrote Wittgenstein   mean the limits of my world

But what did he mean by *language*   and what did he mean by *world*

My grandmother was born in a shithole country and no one recorded her birthday because they did not know the word for *birth certificate* and they did not know the word for *notary* and they did not know the word for *birthday*

They did not know the names of the months and they did not know you were supposed to sing songs on birthdays so no one wrote down her birthday and when she was an adult she decided she had been born in early June because the astrological sign she resembled most was Gemini

The military tried to kill her because she protested the war they waged over the block of ice

They threatened to freeze her in an ice cap

They kept her body in a prison camp on a frozen port and shut her in a hole

She was born in a shithole country that was fighting for the sanctity of a wretched block of ice

She said my own country is the most foreign country I have ever been to

But when night falls it's the most dramatic scene I have ever witnessed

The sun setting over our beaches is a performance that lasts two hours   producing tranquility   nostalgia   and embarrassment

She struggled with self-control

While she was in prison she wanted to gamble but she used self-control

While she was in prison she wanted to weep but she used self-control

When she gave poetry readings she often lied during the Q and A to make her story sound more theatrical

Other times she made it sound less theatrical

Other times she refused to answer any question that wasn't explicitly about the relationship between content and form

My grandmother was a mean woman

She screamed when I woke up in the middle of the night to pee because she would hear me and then she wouldn't be able to get back to sleep

I nearly peed the bed trying to keep her from waking up

I have a small bladder

I'm a terrible sleeper

You have nightmares in poetry   wish fulfillment in prose

It was the night after the president of the World Bank appeared on television to advertise a new sovereign state whose only currency would be cryptocurrency

The head of his lover was sealed in a jar and he wanted the world to see her teeth

He showed us her smile

He said that when she smiles a body in another part of the world feels joy and that soon this will be the future

Other people will smile and this will cause us to feel joy

Other people will control our feelings and we will control the feelings of others

You will cry and someone else will weep

By other people he meant ghosts from dying villages whose names we cannot pronounce

And the next day the value of cryptocurrency skyrocketed and we made tons of money but had no idea where we could find it or how we could use it

I invented this country   said the president of the World Bank   we hardly have time to bury our dead

I invented this country and created revolutionary separatist groups to provide the illusion of tolerant democracy

I knew you when you were just a baby   said the president of the World Bank to his entire viewing audience   though it was the first time we had ever met

They dropped a bomb on the block of ice and the war effectively ended

They dropped the bomb and destabilized gentrification

They dropped the bomb and encouraged entrepreneurial disinvestment

They dropped the bomb and there were foreclosures   grassroots coalitions   community organizations   press conferences in freezing weather and the refugees from one side of the border had no choice but to cross to the other side of the border

Their bodies had lost value even though their potential for labor   in theory   was a commodity

They dropped the bomb on the border and put the most unwanted survivors in the hands of a nouveau-nationalist think tank

The survivors became storm troopers

They became police officers

They slept in concrete warehouses

They destroyed federally funded hospitals

They wiped clean any trace of the border   the bombs   or the block of ice

They studied complex theories of colonialism

They read Plato and Marx and Freud and sang songs about nymphs and centaurs and Wells Fargo and the tangled web of price-variation accounting

They destroyed romantic tenements

They held intense debates about thingification

They picked up our bones like children

They sang songs about the unilateral dominance of lyrical subjectivity

They sang songs about children who resisted the cross-fertilization of the Americas

They studied the agriculture and architecture of the Aztecs and they were cultural emissaries of the state

They sucked on bullets as if they were Mentos

They went on too long about the connection between social mobility and historical poetics

They built temples out of sperm and spit

They spoke to each other in gurgles and murmurs

There was no translation into English

Dream Song #322

A technical error caused the bomb to fall from the airplane and onto the city

The military knew it was a bomb but they told the reporters it was a UFO

The critic believed that because I avoided rhyme and meter I was under the illusion my verbal constructs were self-generated by nature

A spokesman for the mayor apologized for not warning residents the army dropped training bombs in their neighborhood

I lightened the burden of my imagination by casting out the past and all its anxieties

I thought my therapist was a redeemer   but really he was the Antichrist

I wanted to be avant-garde   but I was too concerned with being liked by my audience

I tried to write a sonnet   but instead I wrote a seven-page letter to my grandmother

When I said good-bye to my grandmother for the last time she wouldn't come out of the bathroom because of the germs

She hugged a bottle of bleach   gave me cab fare and I never saw her again

The past is an endless crisis that reappears with each new state of crisis

When she poured bleach into the sink I imagined dead fish in the river or birds falling out of the sky

The city hasn't replaced the corroded water pipes in two hundred years

There are holes where once there was lead

No one drinks tap water

We only brush or bathe when we need to

She told me I needed courage

But what I really needed was a sandwich

She told me I needed grit

But what I really needed was clean water

I remember the hotel room where I saw a man cry for the first time

He was talking on the phone to his best friend   my grandfather   they hadn't spoken in years

The curtains were the color of red wine

The bedspread the color of sand

My grandfather's best friend was traded to another country for petroleum in a plea bargain he never agreed to

I tried to seize hold of the memory at the moment of danger   but I missed

The prisoners in the glaciers were filmed and forced to smile

They sang

The block of ice will always be ours

Shithole Song #1106

we sing it in the blood flowers and we sing it while they bury our sisters

we sing it to the hungry rodents they cage us with

we sing and we sing and there are cannibalized families in the shithole

and the authoritative bodies command us to dig and they say thank the lord we do not live in this shithole where the babies cry for their cages where the mothers have numerical codes stitched into their skin   where the hole is overwhelmed by the shit   and the shit is overwhelmed by the hole   where the hired help helps the hiring hands to rehumanize the exiled bodies whom they shovel into the shittiest shit of the shithole

we are the moses and the aaron of the shithole and we sing this song of hope

we are the mannequins and the glass dolls of the shithole and we sing this song of hope

we are diseased bits of shithole earth on lizard corpses and when our children cry they tell us dig that shithole deeper

they say sing this song of hope and dig that shithole deeper

we sing it to the dead who drink our dirty water

we sing it to the dead who sleep with the ghosts

in our hepatitis hole

in our meningitis hole

in the hole where they hide us like a debt that will never be paid

in the hole where they draw an intractable border through our broken shithole bodies the early Americans tape up our eyes because God tells them to tape up eyes

they chain up our legs because God tells them to chain up legs

they gag our mouths because God tells them to gag our rotten shithole
mouths

they put our children in cages because God tells them to put children
in cages

they dig the shithole deeper because God tells them to dig the shithole
deeper

they slaughter a few grandmothers because God tells them to slaughter
a few grandmothers

heaven is warm bread on every table

heaven is slow breath natural light warm bread on every table

in the shithole we have no bread and we have no table

we are the conquest of the shithole

and the reconquest of the shithole

and the counterconquest of the shithole

our bodies possess collective resonance because we know the global
economy cannot function without the shit and the hole of the shithole

we know the global economy cannot function without the song of hope
we sing to the shithole

we sing into the devices they hook to our bodies

we sing and we sing and sometimes they throw crumbs for us to fight over rain falls into the shithole and they tell us we don't get wet

we are soaking wet but we are not wet because they say we are not wet

we are not wet because God says we are not wet and there are more shitholes hiding in this shithole

they hide our passports in the shithole beyond our shithole

they organize our hunger into units of betrayal in the shithole

soon our shithole will be exported into a less shitty shithole in the prettiest shithole of all the shitholes in texas georgia florida nebraska illinois and new york shithole

we are the prettiest shit in the shithole

we are a people of hope and we sing and sing

we sing as they shit into our shithole

we sing as they shock us in the shithole

we sing as they lend us money to rent back our bodies in the shithole

we are proud to be a people of hope because they tell us we should be proud to be a people of hope

and we sing the song of shithole hope as the souls of our slaughtered classmates fly above our heads

we sing the song of shithole hope as the souls of our slaughtered nurses fly above our heads

we sing the song of shithole hope as the souls of our slaughtered neighbors fly above our heads we sing the song of shithole hope when they shit into the shit of our shithole

we sing the song of shithole hope when they shove poison stones into our wound-mouths

we are the slaughterers' nostalgia in the shithole

we are the murmuring wound-mouths of the rotten bodies that have been blown apart in the shithole

we are the obliterating blankness of the shithole

we sing our song of hope to the massacring minds of the obliterating blankness of the shithole

you are responsible for your wounds   says the authoritative body to the murmuring wound-mouths in the shithole

and you are responsible for your children's wounds

and this is so because I say it is so

and I say it is so because God tells me it is so

and God tells me it is so because I am on the outside of the shithole and you are on the inside

and on the inside of the shithole you are responsible for your wounds and for the wounds of your shithole family

you will be billed for your wounds when the entrepreneurial slaughterers of the morning locate the polytheistic profit in the spiritual marketplace of your ugly shithole mouth

because in the shithole   the death of the dead does not die

because in the shithole   the wound-mouth is stuffed with celebration
cheese and celebration wine

the wound-mouth is stuffed with the impossibility of feeling the feelings
one feels when one cannot contain their shithole feelings

here cometh the form of the shithole

and we sing

protect the concrete from the feet that walk it   cover the concrete with
pictures of the bodies blown apart by the morning   convince the bodies
in the shithole that the slaughterer is not a person

convince the bodies in the shithole that those they slaughtered are
martyrs sacrificed in the communal fight for eternal shithole justice

the river is dying   says the authoritative body to the shittiest shits in
the shithole

the immigrants are flying   says the authoritative body to the shittiest
shits in the shithole

the death of the dead does not die

Identity Theft

His identity was stolen and he needed to reclaim it

He hired a mother to reenact his own birth in the hopes he might find his identity

An old man stole his identity and drove away in a Prius

He hired a mother to reenact his own birth but she did not talk like his mother

A man in Tennessee bought $324 worth of golf equipment with my credit card

When someone steals your identity it is not unreasonable to think it's a crisis

He rented a baby and a nurse to reenact his own birth and filled a hospital room with flowers

There were charges on his credit card for kitchenware purchased on Amazon

He called Amazon to complain and they referred him to their fraud-detection department

If you reenact historical events people will pay money to see this

My colleague dresses up as a Confederate soldier in order to reenact the Civil War

He owns a Confederate frock coat

He owns a Confederate sack coat

He owns Confederate trousers   shell jackets   vests and caps

He plays in a Beatles cover band and often these two identities collide

He sings "Strawberry Fields Forever" in a Confederate frock coat

I felt embarrassed and dejected after spending forty minutes trying to get a historian who sings "Strawberry Fields Forever" in a Confederate frock coat to join the union

But it was easy to get the security guards to join the union

Last month a boy climbed onto the roof and fell off it

There were no guards on duty to prevent this from happening because they had cut the security budget by 59%

The police report spoke of brain matter by the entrance to the school

Neighborhood kids get drunk and climb to the roof and sometimes they fall

I added an extra layer of security to my email account because I was afraid my colleague would steal my identity

I don't know how to say no to people

I gave my friend the password to my cable account so she could watch Showtime and HBO

I didn't trust her but I couldn't say no

I didn't want her to pretend on the internet that she was me

I was afraid she might share my identity with other people

I was afraid that one of these people might sign me up for pornography and sports packages I do not need

He wanted a new identity and at the same time he wanted another crack at his childhood

In elementary school he drank water with lead in it

At home he drank water with lead in it

He believed that lead exposure was responsible for his anxiety and high blood pressure

He believed his mother had lead in her blood during pregnancy

He believed his reduced attention span and antisocial behavior were caused by prenatal exposure to lead

I'm writing this email with tears in my eyes

I came to London for a short vacation

Unfortunately I was mugged at my hotel

They took all my cash

They took my credit cards

I really need your assistance

A famous poet sent me this email and I almost sent him $600 in return

I want a new identity because I have dreams that God will abandon me and I will drown in a lead-filled river

I will rot in the river and no one will find me

My eyes and lips and hair and face will rot in the river

And I will be carried away by vultures

To the corporate headquarters of Bank of America

Where my remains will be exchanged for complex financial products

I will be traded for collateralized debt obligations and mortgage-backed securities

My body will decompose and I will scream

I want to slowly earn interest forever

How I Got Here
An Interview with Espinoza

   —for Kristin Dykstra

I blame my father's father and my mother blames my mother's father
and my father blames my father's mother and my father's mother blames
my mother's mother's father but mostly I blame my father's father and my
mother's mother and my mother and father for procreating

What the fuck were they thinking

Some words stand for some things and other words stand for other things

Or all the words are empty or unavailable

They wrap my body in a flag

They spit on me

They talk about my mother

They blame my mother for making me

They blame my mother for making me a pansy

They call my mother a whore

They call me the son of a whore

They call my father a son of a bitch

I have a memory of my grandfather on stilts in a backyard

I am six years old

I remember laughing with the children as we ran up to the man on stilts

It's possible this is a cheap trick my mind is playing to make him much taller than everyone else

I remember a warm man   a full head of gray hair slicked back over thick square glasses

He knew the president

He had been friends with the president

He formed the party with the president

He started the revolution with the president

My mother met the president at a cocktail party

Too bourgeois?

My mother met the president at an ice cream social

It was a fundraiser for the revolution

They didn't drink wine

They wished they could have drunk wine

They wanted the revolution to have wine but they were afraid that those who could not afford wine would not join the revolution

All the poor people who can't afford wine will soon be able to afford wine   brother

The revolution will guarantee wine for everyone

Let me explain

The president was a nice man

The president offered my mother a job

He said   when you finish law school   join the revolution

He offered her a job with the revolution

My mother was not a Jedi but she knew how to use the force

You will give me a job when I finish law school   my mother said to the president

And the president repeated   I will give you a job when you finish law school

I do not use the force but I am force-sensitive

My mother said   you will give me a job when I finish law school

And the president said   yes I will give you a job   if they don't shoot me first

He was fatalistic

He was kind

He was a quote-unquote   philanderer

Some say he was a great politician

Others say he was a lousy politician

Others think he was ethically dubious because he had sex with young revolutionaries

But then they dropped a bomb on his ass

He killed himself before they shot him

They dropped a bomb on his house

They dropped a bomb on his house but he killed himself before his house went up in flames and now the people pay 25% interest to the capitalist administrators who make a beautiful commission from their privatized social security earnings

This is what Margaret Thatcher meant when she said   economics are the method   the object is to change the soul

I can explain the politically neutral discourse of neoliberal policy

If they hadn't dropped a bomb on some guy on the other side of the world then we wouldn't live in a city with privatized sidewalks   parks beaches   nurses   teachers   trees   weeds   squirrels ducks coyotes

I am trying to convince you not to sell my body on the global market

I am trying to convince you that it's not my fault I was born into a family of communists

Have you seen the way they made my grandfather grovel

There's a movie about this

It's on Vimeo and YouTube and Netflix and Amazon Prime

It's called   *The Groveling Communists*

It stars Gael García Bernal and Penélope Cruz and the prisoners are wretched and good looking

It's about ten communist prisoners on a frigid island who crawl around freezing   dying of hypothermia   trying to teach each other foreign languages in order to keep their brains from atrophying

It's about ten communist prisoners on a frigid island who crawl around in the mud going   *grovel grovel grovel*

I can explain

My mom was like yo president it would be great if you could give me a JOB
after I finish law school and the president was like yeah girl no problem I'll
give you a JOB if they don't fucking kill me before you graduate

My father's father was a revolutionary

But then they excommunicated him from the party

Or he excommunicated himself from the party

It's complicated

He was besties with the president   played ball with the president when
they were in high school   went out drinking with the president when they
were in college   wrote revolutionary treatises with the president over
bottles of wine and cigarettes

But then they had an argument

It's complicated

Like really geopolitically complicated

Sort of

The party loved nation A in a faraway land but my grandfather did not
like nation A because nation A wanted to kill the people of nation B and
the party (though they did not believe in violence) were not fans of the
people of nation B and they supported the people of nation A in their
{impossible} quest to wipe nation B off the planet

The president liked nation A   my grandfather liked nation B

They fell out over this

My grandfather was written out of the revolution and started walking
around on stilts to impress his nephews and grandchildren

He practiced peace but had little interest in peace

He practiced free love but had little interest in free love

He practiced law but had little interest in law

He practiced poetry but had little interest in poetry

SMILEY FACE EMOJI KISSY FACE EMOJI TONGUE HANGING
OUT OF MY MOUTH EMOJI

I am radically resignifying traumatic memory in a diasporic space in
order to create opportunities for new bonds to be articulated beyond the
traumas of dictatorship

Dude

I fetishize the past I did not live

I fetishize the future I cannot control

I fetishize the practical impossibilities of the present

The frozen lilacs   the burning earth   the human beings scorched and
traded for oil

I cannot explain those things

But I can explain other things

The rain is beating on the windows and it really sounds quite pretty

No one will wait for me when I turn into ash and dust

When I am lonely and have no one to talk to I will remember the
murmuring leaves

The Block of Ice Is Ours

The American firearm icon   used to kill a teenage boy   sold for
$130,000 to a mother who wanted to get her son a really cool gift for his
birthday

Because I love you   son   I bought you a really cool gun for your
birthday

I ask him to describe the barracks   to describe the bed on which he
slept   the route he took to get to the bathroom

The bodies were sleeping on the floor   he had to crawl over
them   sometimes they stepped on each other's hands and faces

I ask him about the block of ice and he says he remembers the coffins

They took the coffins to the border so the children would have a place to
sleep when they died

He didn't want to keep telling the story because he was afraid that his
version of history and my version of history would not allow us to love
each other

There was a war that stood in the way of our love for each other   there
was a block of ice that stood in the way of our love for each other   there
was a war in the whites of your eyeballs   there was murder in the whites
of your eyeballs   there were white nationalists in the tearing whites of
your eyeballs

There were borders   there were dollar bills   there was a complex
economy of love-loss and love-gain in the impossible whites of your
eyeballs

I am eight years old   sitting on the bed of a hotel room   listening to the
weeping of a man and a woman who haven't spoken in eight years

They are not happy to talk to each other   they are not happy to hear each other's voices

Why did you take my daughter away   the woman says

The man can't explain that it was history that took her away   that it was the present tense that took them away   that it was the future that took them away   that it was bureaucracy that took them away   that it was accident that took them away

That it was harder to come back than to stay

That it was harder to face a familiar failure than an unfamiliar one

He can't explain that all the countries are terrible

And the woman can't explain that to survive she needs to have a certain faith in the possibility that institutions can and must be rebuilt

Just as the man can't explain that he is not obliged to honor a country that tried to kill him

There is a border in the whites of their eyeballs   there is an excess of love in the whites of their eyeballs

There is an infinite sadness that comes from an excess of love and loss in the impossible whites of their eyeballs

And the man doesn't know how to say   I understand your pain

And the woman doesn't know how to say   you did the best you could

And the historians laugh and the philosophers laugh and the journalists count dead bodies at the border

653 unidentified bodies in the coroner's office and there are no funerals no death certificates   no memorials   no truth commissions for those who die trying to cross the border from country A into country B

I hope you love your fully functional firearm   son   I hope you display
this icon of American history in a prominent place in your dining room

I hope you use it to hunt the boys   says the proud and happy mother

The boys they want to be hunted

The Crisis

The smuggled bodies float into the crisis of a dying continent where the dead children are reproduced like pages off a printing press

The pages blow away and so does the crisis

The analysts believe the crisis must always be inside another crisis

They move the crisis from one network to another   from one currency to another   from one language to another   from one body to another   from one device to another   from one disease to another   from one nation to another

The crisis has appropriated the authority of the state and the bank

It is not the crisis you think it is

It is the crisis of crises

It is all the crises and it is just the right amount

An authoritative body says   we must reproduce human death in order to sustain the crisis

But this does not prevent us from loving your crisis   from recognizing that your crisis has stories and dreams like the rest of us

Once upon a time there was a network that moved the crisis of progress from an old death camp to a new one

But when the crisis got to the new camp the gas chambers were empty   the earth had devoured all the corpses   the crisis was in danger   animals and languages went extinct

But the people kept being born and dying as the futures continued to advance

Take a Body and Replace It with Another Body

Take a word and replace it with another word

>   This is the most miserable place I have known

Take a word and replace it with another word

>   This is the most miserable life I have known

Take a verb and replace it with another verb

>   The river swallowed my face my mouth my body my arms my
>   hands my legs

Take a verb and replace it with another verb

>   The river loved my face my mouth my body my arms my hands
>   my legs

Take a noun and replace it with another noun

>   The authoritative body loved my face my lips my teeth my tongue
>   he loved me

Take a body and replace it with another body, take a verb and replace it
with another verb

>   The bureaucrat killed my face my lips my tongue my teeth he
>   killed me

Take a blank and replace it with another blank

>   The blank blanked my blank my blank my blank it blanked me

The wrong face might kill you

A certain change might be possible if the wrong face kills you

A certain change might be inevitable if the wrong face doesn't kill you

You think you drowned in the river but really it was the city that killed you

You think you are the body that drowned in the river but you are dead
and you do not get to control the circumstances surrounding your
disappearance

Take a word and replace it with three words

> You do not get to have feelings about the circumstances
> surrounding your disappearance

Take a body and replace it with another body

> I do not get to have feelings about the circumstances surrounding
> my disappearance

Take an adjective and replace it with another adjective

> I do not get to have feelings about the circumstances surrounding
> your disappearance

Take a verb and replace it with another verb, take a noun and replace it
with another noun

> You do not get to question the circumstances surrounding my
> reappearance

It was a day he knew he would die an unspectacular death in the river of venomous aloneness

It was a night they knew they would die a spectacular death at the hands of the paramilitary nationalists who were armed by the secret police

It was an afternoon they knew they would survive and be forced to persist in a world where they'd rather be dead

Envy leaked from the mouth and vengeance dripped from the eyeballs

Petroleum dripped from the teeth and plastic straws were shoved into the nostrils

He gave his child a kiss on the forehead

He gave the bank a body that once loved him

Parentheses   but in reality it was hard to have feelings

Parentheses   and in fantasy it was even harder to have feelings

He disappeared unspectacularly into the blank of the American night

Take a body and replace it with another body

      I disappeared unspectacularly into the blank of the American night

Take a verb and replace it with another verb, take a noun and replace it with another noun

      I bloomed unspectacularly into the debt of the American night

Written
After a
Massacre
in the
Year 2018

Written After a Massacre in the Year 2018

> *to see is only a language*
> —Samuel Taylor Coleridge, "Written During a Temporary
> Blindness in the Year 1799"

1. To see is only a language and I can't speak it today.
   They've wrapped a heavy blanket around my face.
   The cops deliver the influenza.
   But before injection they need to wait for someone
   to fix the central heating. No one wants to interrogate me
   until they fix the central heating. I chatter
   with the broken refugees in this prison.
   Our faces wrapped in darkness.

2. A list of frozen bodies. A lost list of unclaimed
   bodies. A lost list of privatized bodies.
   A lost list of bodies they seized. We are the lost
   list but we don't know where they keep us.

3. The border bisecting the infected fumes of the infested
   factories. The utopia of statelessness.
   The utopia of transience. They tell us
   Lake Michigan is the Central America of the Midwest.
   They send us here so we can share hepatitis swabs
   with dirty immigrants.
   Hold on to your DNA, refugee-citizens.
   The only question about life is what does it mean to live it.

4. Financiers selling bodies, speculators selling
   blood and sperm: they slink into the webs of the city.
   They tell me I don't have the right to grieve over
   my own body.
   They tell me   to pray and to grieve is illegal.

5. What did he shout before he massacred the grandmothers?
   What did he shout before he massacred the worshippers?
   What did he shout before he massacred the nurses,

the silent, praying skeletons?
He was on his way to the river the blood would
never reach. He was on his way to the nazi meetup
the blood would never reach. The stock market just opened.
The exchange value of a slaughtered Jew is like
the exchange value of a slaughtered Jew. If your
body is on fire a private firefighter
will put it out much faster than a state one.
The death of a sensuous lung.

6. The song of the ram's horn by the river. The early
Americans march to meet the caravan in the desert.
An authoritative body tells me I can't
disembody my body without disembodying
the collective body's body and if I
disembody the collective body's body
then I will have to disembody the imagined community's
body and if I disembody the imagined
community's body then I will need to ignore
the fields of multiple destruction today.
I dip my finger into a cup of blood and wish
for plagues to destroy the empire. I need to
destroy the nation-state but when will I find the time.

7. The bourgeoisie pay taxes to kill immigrants,
bathe in the cryptocurrency of a bank
that will never exist.

8. The song of atonement at the river sings:
Pray harder and the massacre will go away.
Pray harder and the massacre will not turn into another massacre.
Pray harder and the rich people will become poor people.
Pray harder and the slaughterer will turn into a butterfly.
Pray harder and the thirty million white males with guns
will turn into
               a river of testicles rolling down the street.
When they repossess my body
my heart will soak in petroleum and my mouth

will be a baby in a cage.
The poetry of the shattered bone
               in the flame of the human document.

9. The catastrophe is caressed ad nauseam.
   The greased-up multitudes are not afraid to say
   the same thing over and over again. Death leaks
   from their shoes and the slaughtered Jews are like
   slaughtered Jews. I dream about returning to a
   prayer that doesn't exist. It disappeared yesterday
   when they assassinated the morning and turned
   our life into spectacle.

10. You hid behind the soldiers with machine guns running
    down the street. You were praying for plagues and wishing
    your parents would come out of the building alive.
    The worshippers of the dead trees knew
    where there is a first kill there will be a second.
    Where there is a third kill there will be a fourth a fifth a
    five hundredth. The anecdote destroys the analysis.

11. The emigrants split their bodies into communal
    assets. To assimilate they must stand by the river
    with a prophylactic angel in their hands disguised
    as a rocketing hedge fund. In the rupture,
    in the rubble, in the pathological eye sockets,
    in the counter odyssey of the whites of your eyes,
    in the parliamentary assault rifle, the
    parliamentary machine gun splatter,
    the illegal bodies in cages are painted over
    by the analytics and mathematics
    of the hemisphere. How do you quantify the broken
    toddlers rolling on the ground? How do you quantify
    the murmuring grief of the Americas?

12. Marines medicate mothers and mix their milk with
    mononucleosis. Millionaires multiply
    in the machinery of mourning, manufacturing

mausoleums for martyred Marxists in Mercedes.
Middle managers mistake manipulative
merchants for munificent moralists. A military
massacre on the municipal motorway is like
a military massacre on the municipal motorway.
Metaphysical mayors mediate the mythology
of mystical markets while monitoring the murders of migrants.

My mouth is filled with worms.

Written After a Massacre in the Year 2018

There is no country to claim you when you die inside the word

There is no language to claim you when die inside the cage

The exiled cage breathes death at us

The cage of exile heaves private air at us

Look

Don't speak now

Just look

Breathe   into the mouth of the wound

Dream   into the foreclosure of your death

Look   into the vulture of your wound

Look   into the spider of your wound

Look closely into the algorithm that determines the depth of your wound

Whisper into the cage of exile

You have nothing to lose but this breath

Look

Into the breath inside your breath

Look   into the absent body inside your breath

Look   into the absent I inside your body

Look   into the absent you inside your body

No dust on your body no wound on your body no breath on your body
no word on your body no fat on your body no arm on your body no tongue
no shadow no rupture no breath no thought no cage no exile no word no
code no silence

Look

At the broken shadow in your broken shadow

Look

At the flooded street in your flooded street

Look   into the economy of your absence and whisper into the code you
cannot speak

Look   into the silence of the code

Do not speak directly of the breath

Do not speak directly of the suicide

Do not speak directly of the state that paid the kids to toss themselves
into the river

Breathe the privatized wind   breathe through the foreclosure of your
mouth

Breathe the broken shadow into the broken shadow

Do not take money into the cage or they will kill you before it is time to
kill you

Pray gently into the privatization of your absence

Die gently into the privatization of your absence

Pray gently into the accumulation of your absence

Die gently into the cage where the babies cry in your absence

Pray gently into the puffed-up corpses who grow and grow in your absence

The only breath in this cage is death

Written After a Massacre in the Year 2018

Listen. The eyes that grope the sidewalk want to tell us something. They want to tell us: the pain in your face has meaning. They whisper death into our mouths and they want us to know: the death of our mouths has meaning. They whisper love into our eyes and they want us to know: the obliteration of our eyes has meaning. They puke life into our bodies and they want us to know: the betrayal of our bodies has meaning. The hypocrisy has meaning. The wreckage has meaning. The starvation has meaning. The grief has meaning. The exorcism the void the radioactivity the contamination the wind on our faces the apocalypse the disappearance of the voice the disappearance of the breath the disappearance of the body the sand and the mud have meaning. We pray because we can't scream. We recline because we can't sit. What breaks our bodies: it would have been enough. What feeds our bodies: it would have been enough. What loves our bodies: it would have been enough. And the dead cry out: *Dayenu*.

To take the bullet from the gun. To take the gun from the hand that shoots into the faces of those who mourn the street and the sidewalk. To take the hand from the body that murders the fig tree to defend himself. He obliterates the lilac to defend himself. He blows up the willow to defend himself. He shoots into the trees but sometimes he hits the mourners. He wants their grief to disappear. He wants the sky to disappear. There shouldn't be so many birds in it. There shouldn't be so many insects in it. Let the earth devour their bodies.

One morning a man shoots at the sky and tells it not to mourn so loudly. He shoots into the gardens where the mourners jump, where they dance, where they run. Where they are afraid that they too will disappear into the earth. Like the river that disappears into the earth. Like the love that disappears into the earth. Like the ancient language that disappears into the earth. The earth the children are tossed into when they don't know what massacre they came from.

Written After a Massacre in the Year 2018

The truth commission has nothing to say about the truth today

The truth commission is sick of trying to reconcile bodies that do not want to be reconciled today

I won't worry about the sixteenth century today

I won't worry about the journalist and his chopped-up body today

I won't worry about sexual reproduction today

I won't worry about buying groceries today

I won't worry about decolonization today

I won't worry about the quarantine today

I won't worry about the angel with prophylactic eyes today

I won't worry about my antidepressants today

I won't worry about my dying furnace today

I won't worry about the speculators looking for the financial potential in the caged-up children today

I won't even worry about the cage today

I won't worry about Quetzalcoatl today

Or Cortés

Or the Taino

Or Columbus

I won't worry about lead in the water today

I won't worry about how to write a poem about refugee children and prisoners of war today

I won't worry about the wound the poem must fit neatly into today

I won't worry because this is only the story of a single solitary day

It is the story of a single solitary broken animal

Touch its fur   touch its brain   have a touch of its heart   turn its body inside and out

And the wind is tetanus and the wind is hepatitis and I won't pray today to remember the people who were slaughtered just blocks away

I won't worry about similes today

I won't worry about the literal meaning of my body today

I won't be angry today

I won't be happy either

I won't let anyone see me or hear me today

I need the day to break backwards   I need to run through the glass door backwards

I need the food to go out of my mouth backwards   I need to say fuck you and thank you backwards

I am irrevocably changed by the massacre but I cannot talk about that today

I pray for an endless elegy today

I pray for silence and stillness today

I won't write about revolution or trees today

I won't write about domesticity or the destruction of the global economy today

I will be nothing today

And I will be no one

And I will be a broken mouth

Or a broken body in the shithole fantasy of the shithole solitude of the exploding shithole nation

Written After a Massacre in the Year 2018

Walk past the massacre as if nothing has happened

Ignore the corpses in the plaza

Look away from the tanks when they run over the bodies

Here come the ambulances

Look away

Look away when they kill the ambulance drivers

The ritual dance has just begun

Look away

Look away from the swinging arms and legs

Look away from the eyes in a trance

Do not think about feet or arms or hips

The purification of the body cannot happen in private

When the dancers fall one by one   look away

Do not watch them crawl toward safety

They won't make it   so look away

They won't make it   now look away

When they are beaten with iron paws   look away

When the virus leaks out of their pores   look away

When the bodies crawl out of the quarantine   look away

Look away from the tornadoes in their mouths

Rats crawl over their faces   look away

And in the fast-food parking lots   in the foreclosed alleyways   by the smoking gas pumps

There will be a city of slaughterers with hedge funds in their hands

And they will set fire to the mirrors

And they will set fire to the rivers

And there will be a city of cadavers with radioactive hands

Hands like Molotov cocktails

iPads shoved into their mouths

Cell phones shoved into their mouths

The collective cannot solve your problem   so look away

This is not a prayer for your salvation   now look the fuck away

When the mirror makes you kill   look away

When the market makes you kill   look away

There is the space between the body of the slaughterer and the body it slaughters

There is the space between the skin and the oil that fries it

The grandparents in the cages are exploding

The children in the kill line are praying

Let our love be our love

Let our flesh be our flesh

Let us grow

Let us breathe

Let us stay

Written After a Massacre in the Year 2018

You are mended in the locker rooms of the stadiums they dump you in when your body refuses to die

You are mended in Chicago on a beach that refuses to die

You are mended in Cuba on a beach that refuses to die

You are mended in California on a beach that refuses to die

You are mended in Guatemala on a beach that refuses to die

You are mended in Chile on a beach that refuses to die

The corpses of the Americas die their solar-powered deaths every night you refuse to die

You are frozen in the blocks of ice or melted in the sand holes on the border

The morphine drips through your body   eases the pain in your liver

The life-giving nutrients are jammed into your nostrils

A bureaucrat writes a dream song about the gentleness of the drugs they make you take so the blood will flow sweetly through your body

The privatized vitamins are jammed into your mouth and your lips are numb from the needles that grow in the garden

This is the state where the dead are restored to their death

This is the shithole song of the anesthetic

This is the shithole song of the corpse that refuses its own body

A bureaucrat walks by   holding a cage for a baby

Which department or agency does the cage belong to

What cage manufacturer has signed the most lucrative contract with the municipality

It is unclear if the baby becomes a corpse before or after it is put in the cage

In the scope of the universe   before or after does not matter

Once it might have mattered but in the blankest of times the laws of the desert and the laws of the ice block are the same

The laws of the bomb and the laws of the armistice are the same

You walk through the darkness of the surgery room and search for the end of your body

You carry a bag of stones around your neck and the stones are the state that raised you

You carry a corpse around your neck and the corpse is the state that raised you

Written After a Massacre in the Year 2018

They dream of a massacre that can take place in public and in private
at the same time

They like to watch us as we look into each other's empty faces

They like to hear us say   that was the one I loved

We forget our bondage

We are not yet dead

We are at the border of the before and the after

Soon we will cross through the door and become the subjects of an
endless detective novel that began in the fifteenth century

We are parasites and we will always be silent because silence is the
traditional tactic of our people

We are parasites and we are silent and even when we are dead the
country will remain in our voracious parasite-hands

Why have they protected you for so long   the authoritative bodies
ask us   right before they kill us

Why have they protected your parasitic bodies for so many centuries

They want us to answer this question even though we can only be silent

We dream that if we give the right answer then perhaps they will not kill us

But then they disappear us

And when they disappear us they tell us we are savages with the audacity
to have forgotten our own bondage

You are a voracious colony of parasitic savages who poison the people with your fingers that reek of money

Your fingers are the ghosts of money   your mouths are the ghosts of money   your tongues are the tongues of memory

They shove money into our mouths because they know that even when we are dead we will have the power to control the media and the bank

They take us to the dump and load our bodies into a container with cars that have been obliterated in the toxic dumping ground

They disappear us in the toxic dumping ground

They drop us into the scrap-metal heap

They ghost-wash us in the scrap-metal heap and plaster our bodies against the compressed cars

We are with the metal now and soon they will take us to be recycled

This is the iron waste ground of the industrial dead zone where they stick the parasitic bodies who lived slobbering over money and scheming to control the state

They crush us into the stacked cars and we hear the disappeared cries of the bodies we wanted to become

We are the privatized parasites of death and we will miss ourselves so much when we are gone

They force us to survive   but the shithole won't let us be nothing

The Murmuring Grief of the Americas

It is the end of the afternoon and the sky will soon be purple but right
now the desert light is orange and pink and the painter is able to illustrate
how one side of the cage is in shadow and the other is in sun

The toddler in the painting looks exactly like the living toddler in the
cage only the one on the canvas is naked but for a disposable diaper
that sits high on its waist   the one in the cage is wrapped in a red wool
blanket

On the canvas   in the background   there are pencil drawings of bodies
scattered in the distant sand

They are the bodies of the disappeared   says the painter to the
journalists who are already speculating about the amount of money the
painting will sell for when in the morning it is taken to auction

The bureaucrats have brought me to the border to identify bodies but I
can't understand why they don't know that I am dead

They say   we need you to verify the identities of your comrades   and
when we leave the toddler's cage I am taken to the sand dump to name
the corpses of my friends

I begin to state their names   but I am quickly silenced because the
bureaucrats understand that if I identify too many missing bodies then
there will be certain obligations that the law requires them to meet

Someone whispers

The names of your friends are not the names of your friends and these
bodies do not belong to their bodies

The Murmuring Grief of the Americas

You are on the ground, wrapped in a ratty blanket at the edge of the cage. The interpreter wedges her way into the corner. She sits on her knees, brings her head to your mouth so she can hear the whispers that barely come:

I don't know where I am. I don't know who my parents paid for me to get here.

She slides your hat off so the cameras can see you more clearly. You refuse to open your eyes. It is what you have been instructed to do. But the director is unhappy: with the blocking, the angles, the shadows. He asks the interpreter to tell you to look into the camera as the hat is removed from your head.

The assistants give your wrapped-up body a few rolls. They twist you into the proper position, at which point a doctor asks you to open your mouth, to say *ahhh* while you look into the camera.

This moment here, with your mouth open and the doctor looking into it, is where the scene is supposed to turn. Something transcendent is supposed to happen. But the director can't figure out how to realize his vision. He yells *cut*, then confers with his colleagues about what should flow out of your mouth.

Their opinions differ. One suggests a butterfly. Another suggests a snake. Another a stream of the most beautiful words spoken first in a foreign language then translated by a child with a sweet voice, an adorable accent that perfectly articulates how your body and mouth convert the murmuring grief of the Americas into a currency of empathy, accumulation, and massacre.

The crew meets for several more minutes to discuss what should come out of your mouth after the doctor asks you to say *ahhh*. But the director pauses as soon as the cameras start to roll. He is unhappy about something. There should not be a sunset in the background. There should not be flowers in the foreground.

The world will be dark until we douse his body with light.

End Note

We live in a country of massacre, shaped by a history of white-supremacist massacre, of police-and-state massacre, that rages on into the present.

Perhaps we are always, and have always been, writing after a massacre.

"There are blows in life, so powerful," writes Peruvian poet César Vallejo. "I don't know."

Most of my writing life I have been trying to write poetry that grapples with the various violences we witness, we live with, we absorb.

I have been trying to name the violence clearly and resist its routinization and bureaucratization.

I have been trying, as C. D. Wright says, "not to exonerate or aestheticize immeasurable levels of pain."

I don't know.

I write because I know that I don't know.

On October 27, 2018, eleven people were killed and six wounded at the Tree of Life synagogue in Pittsburgh.

I know the synagogue well.

It is a short walk from the house I grew up in, from the house my family still lives in.

When I was a child we were members of the synagogue.

I became a Bar Mitzvah there.

An old friend's father was wounded and survived the October 27th attack.

Other people my family knew were killed.

As reported widely, it was the deadliest attack on Jews in the US.

I have thought quite a bit about whether or not to mention the shooting in this book.

And given the number of mass shootings and white-supremacist killings, I don't want to give the impression that I think one attack is more significant than another.

I agree with what Raúl Zurita once told me in an interview:

"The apocalypse is not when the world ends; it's when one single person is killed. The entire universe becomes deformed when one single person is tortured."

Perhaps, I think, it would be dishonest to not admit that I, and perhaps less importantly, this book, were definitively changed by the Tree of Life shooting.

And perhaps I am afraid of a communal forgetting, and I want to at least offer a few words to honor the memory of those who died in the shooting.

Joyce Fienberg, Richard Gottfried, Rose Mallinger, Jerry Rabinowitz, Cecil Rosenthal, David Rosenthal, Bernice Simon, Sylvan Simon, Daniel Stein, Melvin Wax, Irving Younger.

And all the love that survives.

Another thing.

Before the white-supremacist murderer killed, he posted on social media about HIAS, the Hebrew Immigrant Aid Society.

He wrote: "HIAS likes to bring invaders in that kill our people. I can't sit by and watch my people get slaughtered. Screw your optics, I'm going in."

He blamed Jews and HIAS for helping Central American migrants and refugees come to the United States.

I didn't know this until after the shooting, but HIAS also helped South Americans in the 1970s, including my parents, when they were migrating to this country.

In my mother's words:

"When we came to New York we needed a lawyer to help us with our immigration papers, and since we didn't know anybody we asked our friend to recommend one. He told us to go to HIAS because they would do all the work for us free of charge. We went to the HIAS office on the Lower East Side, and they did all the paperwork for us. Within a year we were able to get our green cards and initiate the process of becoming U.S. citizens."

—

So much has happened since I finished the first draft of this book at the end of 2018. So much more murder and massacre I don't know I don't know I don't know.

The uprisings that began in fall 2019 against the economic system in Chile and the ways that, predictably, the people on the streets were met by police and military repression. The sense of communal hope that came from imagining a life beyond the poverty and inequality of militarized capitalism. The police and state forces that tried to crush that hope by torturing and wounding thousands, and shooting protesters in the face from close range with hardened rubber bullets that caused hundreds of vicious eye wounds.

The white-nationalist, anti-immigrant massacre of Latinx people in El Paso that killed:

Leonardo Campos Jr., Maribel Hernandez, David Alvah Johnson, Ivan Hilierto Manzano, Jordan Anchondo, Andre Pablo Achondo, Arturo Benavides, Javier Amir Rodriguez, Sara Esther Regalado Moriel, Adolfo Cerros Hernández, Gloria Irma Márquez, María Eugenia Legarreta Rothe, Elsa Mendoza Márquez, Juan de Dios Velázquez, Maria Flores, Raul Flores, Margie Reckard, Alexander Gerhard Hoffman, Teresa Sanchez, Angelina Silva Englisbee, Jorge Calvillo García, Luis Alfonso Juarez.

And all the love that survives.

The pandemic that is disproportionately killing Black, Latinx, and Native peoples.

And the anti-Asian violence we've witnessed.

The names we do not know.

And all the love that survives.

The police and white-supremacist killings of George Floyd, Breonna Taylor, and Ahmaud Arbery.

And all the love that survives.

The mobilizations the police have tried to crush after the white-supremacist killings of George Floyd, Breonna Taylor, and Ahmaud Arbery.

After decades and centuries of white-supremacist killings by the police.

And the victims of police murder we do not know.

We are always writing after a massacre, always writing amid the grief and horror of police and white-supremacist murder.

There are blows in life so powerful, writes César Vallejo. I don't know.

For all the love that survives, and for the names we do not know.

I don't know I don't know I don't know.

LITERATURE
is not the same thing as
PUBLISHING

Coffee House Press began as a small letterpress operation in 1972 and has grown into an internationally renowned nonprofit publisher of literary fiction, essay, poetry, and other work that doesn't fit neatly into genre categories.

Coffee House is both a publisher and an arts organization. Through our *Books in Action* program and publications, we've become interdisciplinary collaborators and incubators for new work and audience experiences. Our vision for the future is one where a publisher is a catalyst and connector.

Funder Acknowledgments

Coffee House Press is an internationally renowned independent book publisher and arts nonprofit based in Minneapolis, MN; through its literary publications and *Books in Action* program, Coffee House acts as a catalyst and connector—between authors and readers, ideas and resources, creativity and community, inspiration and action.

Coffee House Press books are made possible through the generous support of grants and donations from corporations, state and federal grant programs, family foundations, and the many individuals who believe in the transformational power of literature. This activity is made possible by the voters of Minnesota through a Minnesota State Arts Board Operating Support grant, thanks to the legislative appropriation from the Arts and Cultural Heritage Fund. Coffee House also receives major operating support from the Amazon Literary Partnership, Jerome Foundation, McKnight Foundation, Target Foundation, and the National Endowment for the Arts (NEA). To find out more about how NEA grants impact individuals and communities, visit www.arts.gov.

Coffee House Press receives additional support from the Elmer L. & Eleanor J. Andersen Foundation; the David & Mary Anderson Family Foundation; Bookmobile; Dorsey & Whitney LLP; Foundation Technologies; Fredrikson & Byron, P.A.; the Fringe Foundation; Kenneth Koch Literary Estate; the Matching Grant Program Fund of the Minneapolis Foundation; Mr. Pancks' Fund in memory of Graham Kimpton; the Schwab Charitable Fund; Schwegman, Lundberg & Woessner, P.A.; the Silicon Valley Community Foundation; and the U.S. Bank Foundation.

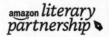
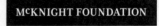

The Publisher's Circle of Coffee House Press

Publisher's Circle members make significant contributions to Coffee House Press's annual giving campaign. Understanding that a strong financial base is necessary for the press to meet the challenges and opportunities that arise each year, this group plays a crucial part in the success of Coffee House's mission.

Recent Publisher's Circle members include many anonymous donors, Patricia A. Beithon, the E. Thomas Binger & Rebecca Rand Fund of the Minneapolis Foundation, Andrew Brantingham, Dave & Kelli Cloutier, Louise Copeland, Jane Dalrymple-Hollo & Stephen Parlato, Mary Ebert & Paul Stembler, Kaywin Feldman & Jim Lutz, Chris Fischbach & Katie Dublinski, Sally French, Jocelyn Hale & Glenn Miller, the Rehael Fund-Roger Hale/Nor Hall of the Minneapolis Foundation, Randy Hartten & Ron Lotz, Dylan Hicks & Nina Hale, William Hardacker, Randall Heath, Jeffrey Hom, Carl & Heidi Horsch, the Amy L. Hubbard & Geoffrey J. Kehoe Fund, Kenneth & Susan Kahn, Stephen & Isabel Keating, Julia Klein, the Kenneth Koch Literary Estate, Cinda Kornblum, Jennifer Kwon Dobbs & Stefan Liess, the Lambert Family Foundation, the Lenfestey Family Foundation, Joy Linsday Crow, Sarah Lutman & Rob Rudolph, the Carol & Aaron Mack Charitable Fund of the Minneapolis Foundation, George & Olga Mack, Joshua Mack & Ron Warren, Gillian McCain, Malcolm S. McDermid & Katie Windle, Mary & Malcolm McDermid, Sjur Midness & Briar Andresen, Daniel N. Smith III & Maureen Millea Smith, Peter Nelson & Jennifer Swenson, Enrique & Jennifer Olivarez, Alan Polsky, Robin Preble, Alexis Scott, Ruth Stricker Dayton, Jeffrey Sugerman & Sarah Schultz, Nan G. Swid, Kenneth Thorp in memory of Allan Kornblum & Rochelle Ratner, Patricia Tilton, Stu Wilson & Melissa Barker, Warren D. Woessner & Iris C. Freeman, and Margaret Wurtele.

For more information about the Publisher's Circle and other ways to support Coffee House Press books, authors, and activities, please visit www.coffeehousepress.org/pages/donate or contact us at info@coffeehousepress.org.

Written After a Massacre in the Year 2018 was designed by
Bookmobile Design & Digital Publisher Services.
Text is set in Ten Oldstyle.